Underst...

The Magic Behind the Law of Attraction

Janet P. Hosmer, PhD

Understanding Universal Laws

The Magic Behind the Law of Attraction

Copyright © 2017
Janet P. Hosmer, PhD

All rights reserved. No part of this book may be reproduced or transmitted in any form or by any means without written permission of the author.

Because of the dynamic nature of the Internet, any links or web addresses contained in this book may have changed or may be invalid.

ISBN 978-0-9857938-0-7

Novus Energia Publishing
Longs, SC

Dedicated to seekers everywhere.

...

Table of Contents

- **INTRODUCTION** 1
- **WHAT MAKES A LAW A LAW?** 7
  - NATURAL LAWS 8
  - MUTABLE AND IMMUTABLE LAWS 10
- **HERMES TRISMEGISTUS** 13
- **THE EMERALD TABLET** 19
- **THE SCIENCE OF BEING & THE KYBALION** 25
- **THE SEVEN UNIVERSAL LAWS** 27
- **LAW OF DIVINE ONENESS** 31

...

- ···LAW OF VIBRATION 35
- ···LAW OF CORRESPONDENCE 43
- ···LAW OF CAUSE AND EFFECT 47
- ···LAW OF POLARITY 51
- ···LAW OF RHYTHM 55
- ···LAW OF GENDER 59
- ···LAW OF ATTRACTION 63
- ···NOW WHAT? 69
- ···RECOMMENDED READING 71
- ···NOTES 78
- ···REFERENCES 87

···

Acknowledgments

In truth, everyone in my life must be thanked, since everything has brought me to here, and spurred the clarity to put this little book together.

Thank you to my "pre-book readers", (Harrison, Maddy, Jolene, Carrie, Margo, David and Cayenne) part of my tribe who understand and live in my "not so conventional" world. I wouldn't have gotten this far without you – and I mean that in so so many ways!

...

How could I not thank my family, who tolerated my 'misunderstandings' as I grew, especially my husband who has weathered, like a champion I might add, all of the bad to get to the good. And as an author himself, has given me wonderful & useful advice.

And my children – a nurse, an educator, and an environmentalist, my girls all continue to cause me delight and growth! They feed my joy as I watch them do all they can to help to bring well being to the world.

However, it's to my boys that I owe the most gratitude. To my very own angel, who chose to remain on this physical plane for only a single day. That trauma, so many years ago, and the quest for understanding that ensued, is what created the deep hunger in me to search for the meaning and workings behind this crazy place we call Earth.

And ultimately to my youngest son and my light, who daily shows me the true meaning of pure love and Alignment!

...

Foreword

Dr. Janet Hosmer has given us a gift -- a primer for helping us understand the seven universal laws -- seven universal truths that have been passed down through various traditions, from Indian to Egyptian to Greek.

Her lofty intention is "to help us understand what governs the Universe" and "to show you how you can easily leverage these Laws. All it takes is changing your mind – really where it all happens."

...

Metaphysical laws are found in a more subtle world. As Dr. Hosmer puts it, "The Laws presented here are beyond our Physical Laws like gravity, because they govern the non-physical, which is where we need to look for explanation and guidance for everything – physical, mental and emotional."

In addition, she explains how the Law of Attraction (LOA) works, something many of us want to better understand. The book puts the LOA into context, showing how it fits into a much bigger picture, and how it interacts with the seven Universal Laws.

In 2006 a movie was released called *The Secret*. It created quite a stir, introducing "The Law of Attraction" to a modern audience of New Agers. I confess the movie left me feeling a bit confused, yet I wanted to know more.

Could creating your own reality be so simple? That is where Dr. H has filled in the void and cleared up the confusion with her gem of a book. She explains the Law of Attraction in simple English -- that what we think and feel goes out into the Universe

...

like a transmission from a radio tower. We get back what we send out.

Then she goes on to show us how we can use the LOA to manifest positive emotions like love and gratitude. Like attracts like. Love attracts love. Anger attracts anger. The Law of Attraction can help us to balance our emotions and live in harmony.

In her book, Dr. Hosmer traces the seven Universal Laws through history, as described by Eugene Ferson in the 1900's in his book, *The Science of Being*. The roots go deep -- back to other ancient texts from Greece and India, including the Vedas, the "books of knowledge" and the sacred wisdom of the Upanishads. She then tells us about each Law, with examples that make it all easy to understand.

After obtaining a PhD in Metaphysics, Dr. Hosmer founded the Life in Balance Spiritual Wellness Center in coastal South Carolina. At the same time, she connected a community of alternative healers and created a metaphysical bookstore and

...

classroom. The center offered workshops, speakers and practitioners providing education and instruction to help those seeking to understand this life experience, and achieve their best and highest authentic self.

Her book is an inspiration, a condensation of her wisdom and deep study of the varied spiritual paths. It is the work of a lifetime in one concise book. As the author so modestly puts it, "This is just a little bedside book giving you the basics of how the Universe works."

Harrison Graves, MD FACEP
Author: *Mantra Meditation: An Alternative Treatment For Anxiety and Depression*

...

Preface

This isn't a self-help book by any means, as there are so many great ones out there. This is more of a historical reference concerning alchemy, ancient Universal Laws, the Law of Attraction, and the origins of many of the beliefs and practices we have incorporated into our day-to-day lives.

At my core, I am a scientist and a teacher. I started my career as a Medical Technologist, studying the human body's chemical physiology, with a desire to help others. Life happened - I changed careers and became a Computer Scientist, understanding and manipulating the working of the digital domain. Ultimately, life tipped me upside down yet one more time, and I needed to understand why! So, I began to learn about the esoteric world of spirituality and energy – possibly where I should have started in the

...

first place? But sometimes we can be slow to catch on!

Long ago, I had a teacher who said that we are only a representation of God's beautiful dream. After years of study, I can clearly see how we do create that lucid and wonderful dream during our time here. But I've also learned that we can only do this by understanding and leveraging the rules of His energetic unseen Universe and connecting the dots.

Now the teacher part.... It is my intention that you, dear reader, use this little book as a quick reference to Universal Law and the Law of Attraction. With it, it is my hope that you can begin to learn how you have, and always have had, the ability to become a true master at creating your own reality.

Please continue searching, learning and growing....

Namasté

Janet

...

···Introduction

Look up at the stars, not down at your feet. Try to make sense of what you see, and wonder about what makes the Universe exist.
Be curious. - **Stephen Hawking**

Universal Laws as well as the Law of Attraction (LOA) have gained wide attention over the last number of years – much has been written, discussed, argued and analyzed. Many have called the perspective of "like energy attracts like energy" a Universal Law, yet many have debunked the whole idea altogether.

Is the Law of Attraction one of the Universal Laws? Some lists say yes ... some lists say no.

Well, that's certainly confusing! It's no wonder so many really don't understand or comprehend the major significance of these ancient philosophies, and most are not aware at all of how these Laws play a significant role in our day-to-day lives. And, they have nothing to do with religious beliefs, so where is one to learn about them?

What are THE time-proven, guaranteed and traceable Universal Laws? How many are there? When did they originate, with whom, and where did they actually come from? How do they work? Why is so little known about them? Who kept the information hidden? Why don't we know about how we can use these philosophies to shape our responses to life's events? Are these Laws what we need to begin to experience that "happily ever after feeling" that we hear so much about? I thought all we needed to understand was the Law of Attraction? Do we really have control of our own reality? So so many questions....

Interestingly enough, many believe that the confusion was planned thousands of years ago to keep the knowledge hidden from the masses. Some believe that it was felt that the people wouldn't be controllable if they knew that they had this tremendous power within them to shape their own lives. Could this be true? We'll trace our findings back to ancient Egypt and see what we can find ....

We'll begin by getting to know the ancient alchemist and sage, Hermes Trismegistus, (known as the god Thohr in Egypt), called the Scribe of the gods. We'll also reference many of the texts of the *Corpus Hermeticum,* and *The Emerald Tablet* containing ancient Hermetic Philosophy, and begin to understand why information so pertinent to our everyday existence hasn't been uncovered before now.

We'll take a quick look at Eugene Ferson's *The Science of Being*, along with *The Kybalion*, a collection of the Hermetic philosophies penned in the early 1900's. Both of these documents thoroughly digest the *The Emerald Tablet*, re-create it into language that we can understand, and generate seven discrete Laws or maxims.

The meanings and philosophy of each of these Seven Universal Laws that were birthed with the Ancients are described next, and then we'll conclude by describing, examining and understanding the Law of Attraction, and how it works! Interestingly enough, we will see how these Seven Universal Laws support and are the underpinnings and foundation for the Law of Attraction. The secret behind The Secret, if you will.

The intention of this little volume is twofold. First, to give you information that helps you understand what governs the Universe. And second, to show you how you can easily leverage the power of these Laws! All it takes is simply changing your mind – really where it all happens – and truly the only thing you have control over anyway! Sounds easy? Not so much. But everything gets easier with information - even alchemy!

Remember, true alchemy is accomplished when thought is manifest into the physical – it is our hope that this little book will help you to understand how to accomplish that very thing.

> **What is Alchemy?**
> Alchemy can be defined as the process of taking something ordinary and turning it into something extraordinary, often in a way that cannot be explained.
> ...

...

...What Makes a Law a Law?

At his best, man is the noblest of all animals.
Separated from law and justice, he is the worst. - **Aristotle**

Alfred Einstein is reported to have said... "As far as the laws of mathematics refer to reality, they are not certain, as far as they are certain, they do not refer to reality."[i] Most laws are like that. And some things that we assume are laws, are not actually laws at all.

Take time for example. Time is actually a man-made construct or agreement that was created in order to provide structure and order to the day, weeks, months and years. Many may think it is, but it's not a law at all – only an agreed upon label and measure.

Natural Laws

Of course, then there's gravity. When we talk about gravity, we know that gravity is a natural phenomenon, (Natural Law), or something observable that is not man-made – just like the sunrise, weather, tidal flow, moonrise, etc. In other words, these are natural or normal occurrences on our planet, and man can't take credit for anything about them.

The Law of Gravity, or the Law of Gravitation, is one of Newton's laws. Einstein's theories regarding the relationship between mass and energy, states that objects with mass are attracted to one another. So together, this explains why something falls from the top of the dresser – because there's a gravitational pull (always!) from the large mass, (the Earth), that has an effect on anything with mass in its physical form on or near the surface.

But how do we come up with laws that exist and have been continually demonstrated within the non-physical or esoteric world? We can't really prove anything, can we? How can we call it a law? Who said? Are these Metaphysical Laws since they describe the nature of reality? Is the Law of Attraction a New Age phenomena, or is it the re-worded and applied teachings of the Ancients?

We know how civil laws are determined in our world, people have to agree, and documents signed and then enforced. But what about Divine Oneness? Or the Law of Cause and Effect? Or the Law of Rhythm? And what about free will? How does that work within all of this?

Mutable and Immutable Laws

Mutable laws are dynamic, changeable and therefore can be transcended, and immutable laws are static, meaning they cannot be modified or changed. Immutable comes from the Latin, *immutabilis*, meaning "unable to change".

When looking at the Seven Universal Laws, there are three immutable Laws, which are sometimes called the Higher Absolute Laws because they function in the Spiritual Plane, and 4 mutable laws which operate in the Mental and Physical Planes and can be overridden. Eugene Ferson calls the three immutable laws, the *Laws of the Absolute* since they cannot be overridden, and the mutable laws are the *Laws of the Relative,* since they are transitory and can be transmuted. [ii]

Our plan to determine validity of these Seven Universal Laws and the Law of Attraction is to follow the breadcrumbs left from scrolls, volumes and texts that have been transcribed and believed and lived for thousands of years.

We'll go all the way back to Ancient Egypt, follow what we find, and we will see how those breadcrumbs lead us to now, and to our part in the creation of reality.

...

···Hermes Trismegistus

> *"The secrets of alchemy exist to transform mortals from a state of suffering and ignorance to a state of enlightenment and bliss."* - **Deepak Chopra**

Hermes Trismegistus, (which means thrice-great) was referred to in many different ways, but always with reverence and awe. Hermes was known as the Scribe of the gods, and has been noted as the premier god of esoteric wisdom, alchemy, magic and the occult. He has been referred to as "The Master of Masters of the masters of Ancient Greece and Egypt."[iii]

Scholars fail to agree on dates for Hermes existence, however some have traced indications of his philosophy and writings as far back as 1,000 BC. Some say he was a contemporary of Abraham and some references date back to the times of Atlantis, and yet others believed that Hermes was older than Moses. Although there is no exacting proof of Hermes existence in physical form, texts have been found in Egypt from Alexander's time that reference Hermes' work, and there certainly can be no denying Hermetic philosophy and its impact on the world.

It was Marsilio Ficino who believed that they called him Trismegistus because he was the greatest philosopher and the greatest priest and the greatest king. Some texts state that this was because he had knowledge of the three parts of the Universe - alchemy, astrology and theology. Others state that it was because of his knowledge of the trinity of God. As a side note, Stanford

Encyclopedia of Philosophy lists Ficino, the first author of theology, among philosophers that first turned from physical and mathematical topics to contemplation of things Divine.[iv]

Hermes was a Grecian god and was often referred to as existing in combination with the Egyptian god Thoth. The two gods were eventually worshiped as one in the same temple. In Ancient Egypt, Thoth was a god of magic and writing, as was Hermes in Greece. Where Hermes was an expert at alchemy, Thoth was reported to have invented medicine, magic and the civil and religious practices of Egypt. Together they were more than powerful.

The combining and worship of two gods together is an excellent example of syncretism or the combining of differing beliefs, traditions and schools of thought. Something to give serious thought to in today's religious climate.

Hermetic philosophy describes three planes of existence - the physical plane, the mental plane, and the spiritual plane – each having a higher vibratory rate respectively, and each communicating with the other two continuously, and reacting accordingly. This in itself is quite interesting, and matter for research in itself indeed.

As an example, you dreamt last night of an eagle, which is representative of spirit vision (spiritual); you are in the middle of a serious conflict with your daughter, and you are unable to "see" that she is in need of help (mental); you have discovered that you are beginning to form a cataract in your left eye (physical). In this case, vision is the issue, and the manifestation can be either positive or negative, since according to the Law of Polarity, all manifestations are truly only 'one thing'.... just in varying degrees along a continuum. But, more of that later....

Hermes is credited as the author of a collection of hundreds of sacred texts where he is portrayed as the master in conversation with his students, as many philosophical works were styled in that time. These texts include the *Corpus Hermeticum* and *The Emerald Tablet*, the philosophical portions of which can directly be linked to the Seven Universal Laws.

Interestingly, Hermetic philosophy shows tracings to Neoplatonic, Gnostic, Pagan, Early Christian, Taoist, Coptic philosophies and beyond. This Ancient Wisdom, with a strong basis in alchemy and magic, and used to unlock the secrets of the world, has been handed down from Masters for thousands of years to Neophytes, who later became Hierophants, Adepts, and finally Masters themselves to continue the process again, and again within the world's religions.

...

⋯The Emerald Tablet

Through consciousness our minds have the power to change our planet and ourselves. It is time we heed the wisdom of the ancient indigenous people and channel our consciousness and spirit to tend the garden and not destroy it. – **Bruce Lipton**

As with most information regarding Hermes and his philosophies, the origins of *The Emerald Tablet*, also known as the *Smaragdine Table* or *Tabula Smaragdina*, are sketchy at best. However, scholars agree that it is first mentioned in texts around 300 AD during Alexander's reign in Egypt.

Although outside the scope of this book, and actually material for a course of study in itself, basically the alchemical principles found in the tablet are believed to contain the secrets of the creation of matter from chaos and the determination of the First Thing or First Matter (prima materia) in alchemy. The generically written text is the uncredited inspiration for many of our spiritual and religious traditions.[v] Many consider the tablet to be one of the earliest of all alchemical works to have survived from that time, and a pillar of western alchemy.

A great many translations of Hermes' Emerald Tablet have been attempted and transcribed throughout the years. The following was found in Isaac Newton's collection in the King's College Library in Cambridge.[vi]

The Emerald Tablet Contents

1. *Tis true without error, certain & most true.*
2. *That which is below is like that which is above & that which is above is like that which is below to do the miracles of one only thing*
3. *And as all things have been & arose from one by the mediation of one: so all things have their birth from this one thing by adaptation.*
4. *The Sun is its father, the moon its mother, the wind hath carried it in its belly, the earth is its nurse.*
5. *The father of all perfection in the whole world is here.*
6. *Its force or power is entire if it be converted into earth.*
7. *Separate thou the earth from the fire, the subtle from the gross sweetly with great industry.*
8. *It ascends from the earth to the heaven & again it descends to the earth & receives the force of things superior & inferior.*
9. *By this means you shall have the glory of the whole world & thereby all obscurity shall fly from you.*
10. *Its force is above all force. For it vanquishes every subtle thing & penetrates every solid thing.*
11. *So was the world created.*
12. *From this are & do come admirable adaptations whereof the means (or process) is here in this. Hence I am called Hermes Trismegist, having the three parts of the philosophy of the whole world*
13. *That which I have said of the operation of the Sun is accomplished & ended*

Hermetic philosophy was prevalent in Europe during the Renaissance and and the Reformation. The 19th Century saw a revival of Hermetic principles when Helena Blavatsky published her *Isis Unveiled* and began the Theosophical Society which included many Hermetic and Neoplatonic principles. Blavatsky considered her Theosophy to be the synthesis of science, religion and philosophy, and believed that this wisdom underlay all the world's religions.

Blavatsky states, "Tradition declares that on the dead body of Hermes, at Hebron, was found by an Isarim, an initiate, the tablet known as *The Smaragdine*. It contains, in a few sentences, the essence of the Hermetic wisdom. To those who read but with their bodily eyes, the precepts will suggest nothing new or extraordinary, for it merely begins by saying that it speaks not fictitious things, but that which is true and most certain."[vii]

Some say that *The Emerald Tablet* is credited as an influence for the best selling book and film, *The Secret*, which is what spurred the interest in the Law of Attraction. The beginning of the movie does show a hidden green stone being uncovered from a tomb, however the stone is never mentioned again. The 'Secret' as portrayed in that production is that our intentions and emotions will manifest in our lives and world if we focus on them.

There is, however, a bit more to it than that!

...

...The Science of Being & The Kybalion

The *Science of Being*, penned by Eugene Ferson in the early 1900's, was one of the first works to describe the discrete Seven Universal Laws derived from *The Emerald Tablet*. Baron Ferson refers to Universal Life Energy as the Source of all creation, and presents a comprehensive and complete understanding of Universal forces and how they interact in the 27 Lessons found within that volume.

It turns out that Ferson was a mentor to William Walker Atkinson, one of the Three Initiates authoring *The Kybalion*. The authors of this particular work maintain that the precepts from the

Hermetic library have never been written down, and the teachings have existed as a collection of truths or principles that were uncovered around 300 AD. They maintained that these axioms were not understandable to outsiders, but readily understood by those students of Hermeticism.

The teachings and maxims found in *The Kybalion*, and those of Hermes in general, dealt in the mastery of mental forces, and the creation of the physical from the non-physical. Contrary to popular belief, alchemy is not about turning objects into gold.

The most profound Hermetic Axiom to arise from *The Kybalion* is that *True Hermetic Transmutation is a Mental Art.* The Hermetists teach that the great work of influencing one's environment is accomplished by mental power, and since the Universe is wholly mental, it follows and is logical that it may be ruled only by the mind, or mentality.

...

···The Seven Universal Laws

> *"It's all about our power to focus consciousness,*
> *which is the great secret of some of our*
> *most ancient and cherished traditions."*
> — **Gregg Braden,**

Opinions actually vary widely when it comes to what philosophies or practices are considered Universal Laws, and how they play a part in shaping our day. One can pick up any number of books or research any number of websites listing law after law, many without any history, background or substance, so the confusion is understandable.

Hidden for so very long, we are just now beginning to understand and uncover the secrets covertly transcribed over thousands of years ago. Among others, references by revered philosophers such as Pythagoras and Heraclitus, are being uncovered, and mentions of Hermetic philosophies are referenced in the scrolls uncovered at Nag Hammadi in the 1950's. The Ancients knew that knowledge was power, but as we're now finding out, that knowledge was not widely shared.

This book focuses on the Seven Universal Laws that have deep roots back through ancient Egypt, Greece and the Vedic traditions of India, and their importance within the Law of Attraction. These Laws, based on the work of Hermes Trismegistus are, in no specific order:

The Law of Divine Oneness
The Law of Vibration
The Law of Correspondence
The Law of Cause & Effect

The Law of Polarity
The Law of Rhythm
The Law of Gender

These ancient teachings, simplified down into seven simple and straight-forward laws, rubrics or philosophical principles, show us how the Universe exists and functions flawlessly in perfect order and balance. With this information, we have the tools and the history to become alchemists ourselves and learn to change our thoughts and our perceptions to achieve a more balanced and satisfying life.

We can do this by understanding both the laws themselves, and how the Law of Attraction acts upon them.

...

... Law of Divine Oneness

"Life, Mind, Truth, Love, Spirit, is All in All" - **Science of Being**

"The Universe is Mental, held in the Mind of THE ALL" — **The Kybalion**

The Law of Divine Oneness (also called the Law of Mentalism) is an immutable law that is often called the Supreme Law, as the other six laws are actually contingent upon this maxim. It cannot be transcended.

Being part of THE ALL is what connects all that is – there is a feeling, or a knowing that we are all connected – and the only way that can happen is if we share a non-physical connection. Quantum physicists are just beginning to scientifically understand the impact of consciousness on energy – or if we in fact are all connected, however followers of Hermeticism has known this since ancient times.

This connection to the ALL is referred to by many different names – your Inner Being, Higher Self, Soul, God Consciousness, and more. When one grasps the true meaning and enormity of the Law of Divine Oneness, perception is potentially changed forever.

The existence of only energy or spirit is something that many find hard to completely grasp or understand. How can consciousness, something completely obscure and mysterious, be what makes up our physical world? The explanation of frequency and the densities and continuum involved are certainly outside the scope of this little book. However, this law is paramount as Quantum Physicists are proving over and over again.

No real mastery of your life experience is possible if you do not understand the mental nature of the Universe. Every manifestation must first be "of the mind" since thought must always precede any physical occurrence, expression or emotion.

Let's take a look at some sayings, principles and everyday maxims that originated with the Law of Divine Oneness.

- ❖ *All is One*
- ❖ *Consciousness is the underlying substance of the Universe*
- ❖ *Everyone is a part of you and you are a part of everyone and everything*
- ❖ *There is no permanent reality, only perceptions*
- ❖ *Energy cannot be created – it can only change form*

...

⋯Law of Vibration

> *"Everything is Vibration"* - **Science of Being**

> *"Nothing rests; everything moves; everything vibrates."* — **The Kybalion**

The Law of Vibration is also an immutable law, meaning that it's influence cannot be changed. Yes, believe it or not, at the sub-atomic level, your desk is vibrating!

Quantum physics has come to discover over the course of the last century, that all mass is hardly any mass at all, is comprised of mostly space, and is vibrating and moving constantly with a specific and discrete frequency. If we apply the *Law of Divine Oneness*, we begin to understand the connection between human consciousness and The All, because we all vibrate together,

Everything and everyone in the Universe is just vibrating at a different frequency. The denser the material, the slower the vibration. We, as humans, are simply a receiver/transmitter of those energies. We experience everything that is manifest in our physical environment by translating the vibrations we receive through our five senses when we see, taste, touch, hear, and smell.

Our emotions also have a frequency. In her audio course *Love or Above*, Christie Marie Sheldon teaches that each emotion has a specific vibration. The vibration of love is at 500, and her teaching is that positive emotions like peace, contentment, and joy are above 500, and negative emotions like, anger, jealousy and sadness are below.[viii]

Of course mental activity must also have a frequency associated with each thought if we remember that all experiences occur in all three planes of existence, and the physical, as the densest of the three planes, is controlled by mental and spiritual. What you believe, and "how your mind works" or your personality is responsible for your mental frequency. Are you kind? Lenient? Maybe you're a little cranky today?

If your emotions are currently at "Love or Above" your response to a situation may be to be helpful, supportive and involved. However, if you are typically operating from judgment, fear or resentment, the response to the same situation would maybe be to act rude or apathetic.

What this means is that each and every thing you do, say or think generates a vibration, in the moment. And that vibration determines your thoughts and ultimately your actions. And that same vibration also determines what frequency you are capable of receiving! This is the exciting part that we'll get to later.

Unclear thoughts, or those that are scattered will generate unwanted life results. Much like the workings of a radio station, the goal is to tune into emotions and thoughts of a higher frequency continually, in order to effect your life experience positively. However, clarity of your vibration is key.

A number of authors and teachers have made attempts to quantify the vibration of human emotions,

Emotion	Frequency
Enlightenment	700+
Peace	600
Joy	540
Love	500
Reason	400
Acceptance	350
Willingness	310
Neutrality	250
Courage	**200**
Pride	175
Anger	150
Desire	125
Fear	100
Grief	75
Apathy	50
Guilt	30
Shame	20

since the discovery that a vibration of a higher frequency provides for a more pleasant and satisfying experience. According to Dr. David Hawkins, on his scale of 1 to 1000 on the previous page, anything calibrated above 200 is desired, and below 200 is a destructive and negative energy.

Abraham-Hicks also provided an Emotional Guidance Scale a number of years ago in.[ix] Their scale, found on the following page, shows Joy at the extreme highest vibration and Fear as the lowest, with many emotional states in between creating the continuum.

However, these scales really only serve as indicators of your feelings, as you truly don't need a number or necessarily a label to understand whether the emotion you are currently experiencing is making you feel satisfied or not. But it does help to know that an emotion that is higher on the scale has more power than an emotion on the lower end of the scale.

Understanding Universal Laws

Highest	Joy/Appreciation/Empowered/Freedom/Love
|	Passion
|	Enthusiasm/Eagerness/Happiness
|	Positive Expectation/Belief
|	Optimism
|	Hopefulness
|	Contentment
|	Boredom
|	Pessimism
|	Frustration/Irritation/Impatience
|	Overwhelment
|	Disappointment
|	Doubt
|	Worry
|	Blame
|	Discouragement
|	Anger
|	Revenge
|	Hatred/Rage
|	Jealousy
|	Insecurity/Guilt/Unworthiness
Lowest	Fear/Grief/Depression/Despair/Powerlessness

In all cases, when considering the effect of how the Law of Attraction acts upon your vibration, the goal is to first become aware of what emotion you are currently experiencing and broadcasting. Then do what's necessary to change the thought that produced the emotion, to one that produces a better emotion or makes you feel a bit more satisfied. But more of this when we talk about the Law of Attraction later.

What are some things that we know about the Law of Vibration?

- *Everything in the Universe is always in motion and emits a specific vibratory frequency*
- *Quantum Physics is beginning to understand that consciousness impacts reality*
- *All vibrations are part of mass vibration and the collective consciousness*
- *Physical plane is the densest plane, so control of emotional & mental frequencies impacts the physical*

- *❖ Higher degrees of positivity on any scale, have direct power over lower degrees of positivity*
- *❖ We cannot change the fact that everything vibrates, but we change the frequency of our own vibration*
- *❖ All things are either growing, dying or changing*

...

⋯Law of Correspondence

*"The same law governs always everything, everywhere,
in the same way, from the greatest star
down to the smallest electron. -* **The Science of Being**

"As above, so below; as below, so above." — **The Kybalion**

The Law of Correspondence is also an immutable Law that is the birthplace of "As Above, So Below". This can also be phrased, "As it is in the Inner World, it is in the Outer World". There is always a back and forth and balance between opposing ends of any object emotion or thought and of course, also between the three planes of existence. This one simple statement about the Law of Correspondence also references and relies upon the Laws of Polarity and Rhythm which are described below.

The beauty of this Universal Law is that one is able to determine circumstances in their mental plane by examining the physical or spiritual plane, and the reverse. In other words, one can study and learn about what they do not know by observing what they do know.

The *Corpus Hermeticum* mentioned earlier in this volume focuses almost entirely upon this Law. Hermes firmly believed and taught that everything manifest was represented in all three planes of existence. Thus his, and alchemists of his time, quest to move an experience from the spiritual and mental planes to the physical plane. The current Mind-Body association and movement is based solely upon the Law of Correspondence.

Since we know via The Law of Vibration that the spiritual and mental planes vibrate at a higher frequency than the physical plane, this is certainly possible. Certainly outside the scope of this book, researchers are now becoming aware that our mental health including our emotions does in fact affect our physical health.

Some things to think about when pondering this Law:

- ❖ *As Above, So Below – As Below, So Above*
- ❖ *As Within So Without – As Without So Within*
- ❖ *To Know One is to Know All*
- ❖ *Experiences on One Plane Happen on All Planes*

...

...Law of Cause and Effect

"Every Cause has its Effect; every Effect has its Cause; everything happens according to Law; Chance is but a name for Law not recognized; there are many planes of causation, but nothing escapes the Law." — **The Kybalion**

"Every Effect has its Cause, and Every cause has its Effect"
— **The Science of Being**.

The Law of Cause and Effect is quite commonly understood in today's vernacular. However, the Hermetic philosophy takes it to a different level altogether. It is an immutable Law, and cannot be transcended.

From the Kybalion, "A careful examination will show that what we call 'Chance' is merely an expression relating to obscure causes; causes that we cannot perceive; that we cannot understand."[x]

Chance or luck and terms like coincidence are words and expressions used by people who aren't aware of this law, because those types of experiences plainly do not exist. A coincidence is in fact, where two points converge or coincide, or a cooperative incident – not a chance happening at all. Every occurrence has a cause, whether on the physical, mental or spiritual plane.

You can certainly see how Newton's first law of physics, regarding force and inertia, stems from this Universal Law. Of course, you can see the effect across planes as well if you look carefully. A sour mood, which naturally lowers your vibration, will eventually manifest in a physical experience, whether in your body or your environment, that certainly is the mirror effect of that mood. And the opposite is also true, physical beauty, such as a vibrantly colorful flower garden, will undoubtedly boost your emotions and your state.

The Universe is fair, and always generates back an equal measure of what is given.

Karma is a word that's tossed around quite a bit today. Many definitions exist but the following seems to have the best description without using the actual Sanskrit translation, "The law of cause and effect forms an integral part of Hindu philosophy. This law is termed as 'karma', which means to 'act'.[xi] The Concise Oxford Dictionary of Current English defines it as the "sum of person's actions in one of his successive states of existence, viewed as deciding his fate for the next".[xii]

Sayings, principles and maxims stemming from the Law of Cause and Effect are:

- ❖ *Every Effect has a Cause and Every Cause has an Effect*
- ❖ *A Cause on one plane can generate Effect on another*
- ❖ *You Reap what you Sew*
- ❖ *Do unto others as you would have them do unto you*

...

...Law of Polarity

"Everything in this world in the present state of human consciousness appears to have two poles, the positive and the negative poles"
– ***The Science of Being***

"Everything is dual; everything has poles; everything has its pair of opposites; like and unlike are the same; opposites are identical in nature, but different in degree; extremes meet; all truths are but half-truths; all paradoxes may be reconciled." — ***The Kybalion***

The Law of Polarity is the first of the mutable laws, meaning that it can be transcended. All experiences, in all three planes, have two ends or poles. You have the ability to move along the train track of these poles, and wherever you are on the track determines the experience you will have. In other words, everything in the manifest Universe is only one **thing**, with varying degrees along the continuum with two opposing, yet connected vibrations. Each of these poles vibrates at a different rate, however it is still only one manifestation, object or subject.

This law tells us that everything and anything can be split into two experiences, and that all things come in pairs. All things manifest and un-manifest are relative in nature and are subject to definition. One pole is always the absence of the other.

Dark is simply the total absence of light, but both are the same thing ... simply the eye's response to an emitted vibration (light) with varying shades (frequencies) in between. In fact, the only thing that gives 'dark' any meaning is the existence of 'light'. The only thing that gives music of any kind meaning, is silence. Sound, temperature, texture, odor, flavor – are all translations of frequencies by our human physical senses – and all ruled by the Law of Polarity. Where's the line when hot changes to cold, I wonder? Or stinky to fragrant? Confusion must exist to know clarity.

And the kicker is that this polar opposition can take place across planes! The Kybalion states, "The teachers claim that illustrations of this Principle may be had on every hand, and from an examination into the real nature of anything. They begin by showing that Spirit and Matter are but the two poles of the same thing, the intermediate planes being merely degrees of vibration. They *show* that THE ALL and The Many are the same, the difference being merely a matter of degree of Mental Manifestation."[xiii]

In Chinese philosophy the Yin / Yang symbol is a perfect example of how both light and dark (however each includes the other) work together. This simple symbol describes how seemingly opposing forces can actually be complementary to complete the whole.

And remember, this is the first of the Mutable Laws, meaning that the current state of what is being experienced is changeable. Positive thinking is only moving along that continuum along to the other end of the pole.

Think about the Law of Polarity and how your mental state moves from one end of the pole to the other when the following sayings come to mind.

- ❖ *There's always a bright side*
- ❖ *Every cloud has a silver lining*
- ❖ *One man's trash is another man's treasure*
- ❖ *When one door closes another door opens*

…

...Law of Rhythm

"Everything in the world, in the present state of human consciousness, inhales and exhales, goes up and down by compensated oscillations."
— ***The Science of Being***

"Everything flows out and in; everything has its tides; all things rise and fall; the pendulum-swing manifests in everything; the measure of the swing to the right, is the measure of the swing to the left; rhythm compensates." — ***The Kybalion***

Also called *The Law of the Pendulum*, this law states that all objects are always moving back and forth, in and out, up and down – in a forever dance that continues to renew its energy with each pulse. The Law of Rhythm is a mutable law which allows for the stopping or slowing of the momentum that is moving the pendulum, if it is heading in a direction not wanted along the continuum of the pole.

This Law, which is closely related to the Law of Polarity, is responsible for change, since if it were not for the compensating swing of the pendulum between the two poles of a pair of opposites, nothing would change or expand.

Again, referring to Newtonian physics, Newton stated in his Third Law regarding force that forces always occur in pairs - if Object A exerts a force (F) on Object B, then Object B exerts an equal and opposite force (-F) on Object A. (This particular law also seems to satisfy the Law of Polarity as well).

This rhythm of the forces adheres to the Universal Law of Rhythm, and is one of nature's ways of balancing everything and maintaining harmony.

We've all seen and enjoyed those fascinating and mesmerizing desk toys that has swinging balls called Newton's Cradles – you can thank the Law of Rhythm and think back to ancient Greece.

Sayings, principles and maxims stemming from the Law of Rhythm are:

- ❖ *There is constant flow*
- ❖ *Rise and Fall ... In and Out*
- ❖ *Back and Forth (between Planes of Existence too!)*
- ❖ *Easy Come Easy Go*

One can easily see how the laws of both Rhythm and Polarity apply to manifestations in the physical world. Of course these laws also apply to our mental and emotional selves as well, since movement and momentum occur in both our thoughts and emotions. The key is to become aware of the beginning of the downward swing in any area of your life, and do what's necessary to start the movement back in the desired direction..

Depending on the power of the momentum of the thought, you can change your perception of the situation by "thinking a better thought", or you can change your focus entirely to something more enjoyable and satisfying. Either way, you start the pendulum of your emotions, (which are directly related to the thoughts that you are thinking), towards a better feeling place.

...

...Law of Gender

"Everything in this world in the present state of human consciousness has two genders, the male and the female gender.
– ***The Science of Being***

"Gender is in everything; everything has its Masculine and Feminine Principles; Gender manifests on all planes." — ***The Kybalion***

Gender is a set of behaviors learned through nurturing and cultural interaction. Gender is more complex than a simple biological definition of sex. Gender refers to masculine and feminine rather than male and female.

There is always a masculine and feminine aspect to everything – without such there can be no re-birth. Everything manifest is created via the masculine and feminine aspects of all three planes of existence.

The word "gender" stems from the Latin *generare*, which means to bring forth or generate. Therefore, gender is ultimately responsible for creation and for the expansion of all that is. Also, we must understand that gender refers to the cultural differences expected (by society and a certain culture) of men and women.

Everything in the organic Universe is expressed through gender - all animals, plants, electrons, style, emotions, and on and on. The table on the following page shows a list of masculine and feminine principles and ideologies found in The Adventure of I.[xiv]

As you can see, both masculine and feminine principles

and personality traits are necessary for balanced creation. And again, other Laws come into play here - there can't be a Leader without a Follower, Passive has no meaning without Active, and so on. Interestingly enough, this is the example of the Law of Polarity.

These are the things to remember when thinking of the Law of Gender...

MASCULINE	FEMININE
FATHER	MOTHER
DIRECTIVE	CREATIVE
LEADING	FOLLOWING
PROJECTIVE	RECEPTIVE
PROTECTIVE	NURTURING
ACTIVE	PASSIVE
OBJECTIVE MIND	SUBJECTIVE MIND
WILL	INTUITION
REASON	EMOTION

- ❖ *Gender is in everything*
- ❖ *All manifest objects have masculine & feminine aspects*
- ❖ *What's Good for the Goose is Good for the Gander*
- ❖ *Yin / Yang Represents Masculine & Feminine*

...

··· Law of Attraction

"That which is like unto itself is drawn" – **Abraham-Hicks**

And now we come to the Law of Attraction (LOA), is a New Thought philosophy. In the scientific and energetic sense – it simply means that like frequencies are attracted to one another. This means absolutely nothing and isn't useful at all, unless you understand Hermetic philosophy and the Seven Universal Laws described here.

What it does mean to anyone wanting to change a particular circumstance, is that we can use our ability to control our thought processes with the focusing ability of our minds to enhance our life experience. Why? Because...

- ❖ *EVERYTHING manifest and un-manifest is energy and accessible to us all according the the Law of Divine Oneness*
- ❖ *EVERYTHING also has a discrete frequency, according to the Law of Vibration*
- ❖ *EVERYTHING has a cause, according to the Law of Cause and Effect*
- ❖ *EVERYTHING moves along a continuum according to the Law of Polarity*
- ❖ *EVERYTHING has momentum according to the Law of Rhythm*
- ❖ *EVERYTHING in our physical experience is accessible via our mental capacity to focus according to the Law of Correspondence*
- ❖ *Co-creation relies on the Law of Gender*

Law of Attraction has been dubbed a pseudoscience by some and mumbo jumbo by others. Some references call this a

Universal Law, and some do not. However, if in this work, we are to limit our discussion of Universal Laws to only those discovered and embraced through *The Emerald Tablet*, created so many years ago, then we may be overlooking one of the most important aspects of these Laws – which is how they all work together, and are managed within our Universe.

The Law of Attraction simply states that *Like Attracts Like*, and is certainly not about bringing more tangible items into your life, although this is quite possible once understanding is accomplished. Many teachers and authors have penned volumes on how we create our own reality with our thoughts.

LOA is responsible for personal vibratory management, and the response to one's vibrational offering, thus providing the expansion and evolution throughout the Universe. We humans may deem that expansion positive or negative, but expansion must in fact occur.

On a personal level, our emotions, and "how we feel", indicate the vibration or frequency from which we are operating. This frequency also is broadcast as your current point of attraction. Of course, the better the feeling or level of satisfaction with your current, (in the moment) experience, the higher the frequency that you are transmitting to the Universe. Please see the chapter on the Law of Vibration.

It works like this.... Let's use the Abraham-Hicks scale in our example. If your current, (that means instantaneous) frequency is in the range of *Contentment*, and you stay that way, then the experiences that are available to you will generate that same feeling of *Contentment*. However, if you are currently *Discouraged*, and you focus on being discouraged for any amount of time, the experiences that come into your life will potentially generate that same feeling of *Discouragement*. Your goal, according to the

Abraham-Hicks scale would be to try to find a subject, (not necessarily the one that is making you discouraged) that will make you more satisfied, and bring a higher vibration into your experience... even *Doubt* would be better than *Discouraged*.

Understanding the Law of Polarity helps to clear up how this works. One certainly can't go from Discouragement to Joy immediately – that jump is too far along the continuum of frequencies. Remember, LOA is always at work pulling you to where you are. But if you can re-focus to another subject, (grab a kitty if you have one, or listen to a particularly enjoyable song) – or move up just a tiny bit on the scale in the same subject, (*discouraged* about your job, could turn to *hopeful* about the prospect of getting another) you ultimately have access to better thoughts, even if just for a little while, and better emotions.

Baby steps for sure, but steps regardless, and they should be celebrated!

Cognitive Therapy utilizes Law of Attraction techniques when situations and thought-processes are "re-framed" in order to move forward. The re-framing allows the patient to focus more on the positive end of the situation or experience rather than the negative, since all subjects have two poles according to the Law of Polarity. And since our perception determines our emotion, when we experience a negative emotion, if focus is changed to a more beneficial thought along the continuum, (Law of Polarity & Rhythm) relief from negative thought processes may be achieved by being at the end of the 'pole' that creates more enjoyable emotions.

...

...Now What?

Joy in looking and comprehending is Nature's most beautiful gift.
― **Albert Einstein**

There is certainly more to learn!! This is just a little mini reference book giving you the basics and a quick historical record of the foundations of how the energetic Universe. There are volumes and volumes available for you to explore in order to learn how to really put all of this into practice in your life!

The laws presented here are beyond our physical laws like gravity, because they govern the non-physical, which is where, if we do believe in anything at all outside of our human selves, we need to look for explanation and guidance for all things physical, mental and emotional. The laws described here can be traced back through antiquity, and are without doubt THE Laws of the Universe, finding their way into the underpinnings of many, if not all of the world's current religions.

And the Law of Attraction, acting as the governor and the manager of vibratory movement and expansion throughout the Universe, provides a mechanism for leveraging the power of these Laws and consciously creating reality.

Knowing and using the outcome of all circumstances based on these Laws, provides a solid and irrefutable framework for a belief system providing for the expansion of you and our Universe, in a manner that is balanced and thriving at its core. It takes practice, and awareness of your thoughts – but mostly it takes simply caring about how you feel in order to get started feeling just a little more satisfied with your life experience.

...

··· Recommended Reading

A great number of books and texts were found stating that theirs were the Universal Laws to be followed, therefore research for this book proved to be quite interesting. The following volumes are those that were eventually referenced for the information found within. It is this author's hope that this course will inspire you to find additional resources as your interest and knowledge grows in this field.

The Hermetica: The Lost Wisdom of the Pharaohs (1997) by Time Freek and Peter Gandy is basically an introduction to ancient literature and spirituality, giving a cursory look at the Hermetica using mostly examples from other sources. This book is a collection of excerpts from a number of texts of the Alexandrian Gnostic era, mostly from the Corpus Hermeticum, however is not a direct translation any of the texts cited. (ISBN: 978-1585426928)

***The Science of Being: Teachings of Eugene Ferson (**2011) by Lightbearers Publishing, LLC. Baron Eugene Ferson came to the United States from Russia in the very early 1900's and began teaching his philosophies, eventually mentoring many great names in both science and philosophy. His was one of the first works to bring forth the 7 Universal Laws. His original *Science of Being* (1923) is a collection of his teachings that were channeled via Universal Life Energy, and form the basis of many spiritual teachings today. Baron Ferson was also a mentor to William Walker Atkinson, one of the anonymous Three Initiates, who are authors of *The Kybalion*. (ISBN: 978-0615913087)

The Kybalion: A Study of the Hermetic Philosophy of Ancient Egypt and Greece (1908) by Three Initiates. In this complete representation of Hermetic philosophy, the Three Initiates, who prefer to remain anonymous, assemble Hermetic doctrine into 7 compelling and convincing principles, providing practical methods for applying these ideas and maxims for self-development in everyday life. The purpose is to provide the student with the tools necessary to unlock the great mysteries of the Universe, as they believed that Hermes held the secrets, since the fundamental and basic teachings embedded in the esoteric teachings of every race, religion and culture may be traced back to Hermes. (ISBN: 978-1603864787)

The Emerald Tablet: Alchemy for Personal Transformation (1999) by Dennis William Hauck. This is a book exploring the works of many previous scholars and teachers regarding The Emerald Tablet and the topic of Alchemy itself. This is a text for the serious alchemist at heart, as it delves quite deeply into the inner workings of the craft. Hauck writes and lectures on the universal principles of physical, psychological, and spiritual transformation. (ISBN: 978-0140195712)

Universal Laws: Unlocking the Secrets of the Universe, (2016) by Creed McGregor. A beautiful little book containing a brief description of the natural laws of the Universe and the Law of Attraction. McGregor sites many useful and applicable techniques for putting the laws of the Universe into effect in your life. (ISBN: 978-1530189960)

Twelve Universal Laws: The Truth That Will Transform Your Life, (2007) by Anne E. Angelheart. This is another good book that describes laws that govern the Universe. Angelheart describes 12 Universal laws, each providing for a better life experience once understood and leveraged. Her book includes the Laws of Action, Compensation, Attraction, Transmutation of Energy and Relativity along with the Seven Universal Laws derived from Hermes' Emerald Tablet. Also included are exercises to help along the way. (ISBN: 978-1452536972)

The Adventure of I: A Journey to the Centre of Your Reality, (2013) by Tania Kotsos. This book presents a complete guide for getting to know yourself and put ideas and procedures into practice that will help to enhance your life. Kostos blends together both Eastern and Western philosophy bringing the topic of creating your own reality to many who have previously been much too confused to move forward. (ISBN: 978-0957677005)

The Law of Attraction: The Basics of the Teachings of Abraham, (2006) by Esther and Jerry Hicks. On the Leading Edge when creating your own reality is concerned, Esther & Jerry Hick along with Abraham, their "Infinite Intelligence" mentor and teacher, have put together a question / answer type book covering all aspects of creating your own reality. This book expands more than any of the others on the Law of Attraction, the science of deliberate creation, and the art of allowing. (ISBN: 978-1401912277)

Ask and It is Given: Learning to Manifest Your Desires, (2004) by Esther and Jerry Hicks. One of a series of books written by Esther and Jerry Hicks presenting the philosophy of "Abraham" the non-physical entity channeled by Esther. A place to find the powerful and life-changing teachings of Abraham in an easy to follow and direct presentation. (ISBN: 978-8190416948)

Jack Canfields Key to Living the Law of Attraction: A Simple Guide to Creating the Life of Your Dreams by Jack Canfield, (2007). A guide book on how to put the Law of Attraction into practice in your life. Canfield is known for his Chicken Soup for the Soul series, and has been teaching and lecturing for many years on the benefit of using LOA when creating your own life. (ISBN: 978-0757306587)

...

···Notes

Notes

Notes

Notes

Notes

Notes

Notes

Notes

···References

---

[i] http://www.searchquotes.com/quotation/As_far_as_the_laws_of_mathematics_refer_to_reality%2C_they_are_not_certain%3B_and_as_far_as_they_are_cer/232043/

[ii] Eugene Ferson, *The Science of Being*

[iii] Tania Kotsos, *The Adventure of I: A Journey to the Center of Reality*

[iv] https://plato.stanford.edu/entries/ficino/
[v] Dennis Hauck, *The Emerald Tablet: Alchemy for Personal Transformation*
[vi] https://prezi.com/ort-oii-ltwk/isaac-newtons-translation-of-the-emerald-tablet/
[vii] Helena Blavatsky, *Isis Unveiled*
[viii] Christie Marie Sheldon – Love or Above
[ix] Esther and Jerry Hicks, Ask and it is Given
[x] Three Initiates, *The Kybalion: A Study of The Hermetic Philosophy of Ancient Egypt and Greece*
[xi] thoughtco.com
[xii] First Edition (1911): *The Concise Oxford Dictionary of Current English*,
[xiii] Three Initiates, *The Kybalion: A Study of The Hermetic Philosophy of Ancient Egypt and Greece*
[xiv] Tania Kotsos, *The Adventure of I: A Journey to the Center of Reality*